Other titles in the *Authors Teens Love* series:

Ray Bradbury
Master of Science Fiction and Fantasy
7660-2240-4

. S. Lewis
Chronicler of Narnia
0-7660-2446-6

Joan Lowery Nixon
Masterful Mystery Writer
0-7660-2194-7

R. L. Stine
Creator of Creepy and Spooky Stories
0-7660-2445-8

J. R. R. Tolkien
Master of Imaginary Worlds
0-7660-2246-3

E. B. White
Spinner of Webs and Tales
0-7660-2350-8

Roald Dahl

AUTHORS TEENS LOVE

Roald Dahl

Author of *Charlie and the Chocolate Factory*

Michelle M. Houle

Enslow Publishers, Inc.

40 Industrial Road   PO Box 38
Box 398   Aldershot
Berkeley Heights, NJ 07922   Hants GU12 6BP
USA   UK

http://www.enslow.com

Library of Congress Cataloging-in-Publication Data

Houle, Michelle M.
    Roald Dahl : author of Charlie and the chocolate factory / by Michelle M. Houle.
       p. cm. — (Authors teens love)
    Includes bibliographical references (p.   ) and index.
    ISBN 0-7660-2353-2
    1. Dahl, Roald—Juvenile literature. 2. Authors, English—20th century—Biography—Juvenile literature. 3. Young adult fiction, English—History and criticism—Juvenile literature. I. Title. II. Series.
    PR6054.A35Z695 2006
    823'.914—dc22

                                     2005014914

Printed in the United States of America

10 9 8 7 6 5 4 3 2 1

To Our Readers: We have done our best to make sure all Internet Addresses in this book were active and appropriate when we went to press. However, the author and publisher have no control over and assume no liability for the material available on those Internet sites or on other Web sites they may link to. Any comments or suggestions can be sent by e-mail to comments@enslow.com or to the address on the back cover.

Cover Illustration: Mark A. Hicks (background); Everett Collection, Inc. (foreground).

Photos and Illustrations: All images courtesy of the Everett Collection, Inc., except p. 24, Jupiter Images Corporation, and p. 53, AP/Wide World Photos.

Contents

Chapter 1

A Child at Heart

Charming. Imaginative. Brave. Ambitious. Rude. A doting father. A cantankerous guest. A loving son. A difficult man.

All of these labels could describe Roald Dahl, one of the most beloved children's writers of all time. His stories are well known by children around the globe—*Charlie and the Chocolate Factory*, *James and the Giant Peach*, *Matilda*, *The BFG*, to name just a few. The charm and occasional irreverence displayed by his heroes are qualities he was famous for himself, and he reveled in such fame. Whether he was telling stories to his own children in their fairy-tale-like home in Great Missenden, England, or entertaining millions of readers throughout the world with his novels,

Roald Dahl had an uncanny ability to delight and enthrall children and adults alike.

Dahl wrote twenty-one children's books and dozens of stories for adults. Millions of copies of his books are in print in dozens of languages including French, German, Russian, Chinese, and Japanese. He was published in such magazines as *The New Yorker*, and he wrote screenplays for several Hollywood movies.

In addition to his writing career, as a young man Dahl traveled to Africa to work for Shell Oil; fought as a British Royal Air Force pilot in World War II; and mingled with high society in Washington, D.C., New York, and London. As a family man, he was married twice, to two charismatic women, and had five children and three stepchildren. He had moments of great happiness, but also suffered from numerous tragedies.

Dahl sought adventure and fame, and found both. And despite his sometimes surly demeanor, he is often described as a modern-day Pied Piper.

Roald Dahl died on November 23, 1990, at age seventy-four. He is buried on a hill near his longtime home in Great Missenden. Fans continue to visit his grave to pay their respects to their favorite storyteller. His books are a lasting reminder of the "Great Man," as his daughter Tessa described him, who was truly a child at heart.[1]

Chapter 2

A Passion for Sweets and Adventure

"If I were a headmaster, I would get rid of the history teacher and get a chocolate teacher instead and my pupils would study a subject that affected all of them."[1]

As a small boy, Roald Dahl's passion for candy was as strong as any child's, though his love of chocolate did not begin in earnest until he was a teenager. Like many children growing up at that time, as a young boy he longed for candy (or "sweets" as they were called in Great Britain), rather than chocolate simply because there were not that many chocolate bars available like there are today. Later, Dahl remembered that he and the other children liked to spend their pocket money on all kinds of candies that could be found at the local candy store. Young Roald's favorites were sherbet-suckers, which were tart candies that dissolved slowly in his mouth, and licorice bootlaces, which were long thin tasty strips of licorice that were fun to play with too.[2]

As a young boy growing up in Llandaff, Wales, Roald had several school friends whose passion for sweets was equal to his own. Every day after school, this young crew of boys would make their way to the village sweetshop before going home, and there they would spend what money they had from their allowances on candies of all sorts. This sweetshop was the most important thing in the lives of these young boys. "To us, it was what a bar is to a drunk, or a church is to a Bishop," Dahl later wrote.[3] There was a frightful terror awaiting the children at this shop though, and that terror was the shop's owner, Mrs. Pratchett.

> **Roald had several school friends whose passion for sweets was equal to his own.**

Mrs. Pratchett was a loathsome woman with skinny legs and dirty fingernails, according to *Boy*, Dahl's autobiography for children. She was horribly mean to the children and accused them of stealing sweets and playing tricks on her when she was not looking. Her horridness might have scared away many adult customers, but the children did not care. They just wanted the sweets—and revenge. It was this revenge, however, that provided the boys with the greatest adventure they had ever had in their young lives.

One day, the boys found a dead mouse at school and decided to trick Mrs. Pratchett by dropping its body into a jar of gobstoppers. To do this, the boys devised a plan to distract Mrs. Pratchett while Roald slipped the mouse into the jar. Once this was done, the boys raced home, thrilled with their success. Unfortunately, the joy was short-lived because Mrs. Pratchett was very angry, and she was able to point out the culprits the next day. At school, the boys received a terrible beating as punishment for their crime. Somehow, this did not diminish their love of sweets. It just hardened their resentment of the dreaded Mrs. Pratchett.[4]

As a teenager, Dahl had the good fortune of going to school near the great Cadbury's chocolate factory. In *Boy*, Dahl describes how the boys at the school were occasionally given a box of chocolates by the candy makers at Cadbury. In exchange for this lovely gift, all the boys had to do was explain why they did or did not like the candy. It was a wonderful treat for the boys who were used to plain boarding school food and who all had a passion for sweets. Dahl remembered it fondly: "All of us entered into this game with great gusto, sitting in our studies and nibbling each bar with the air of connoisseurs, giving our marks and making our comments."[5]

It was at school, then, that Dahl received his

Dahl's river of chocolate, as seen in the 2005 film version of
Charlie and the Chocolate Factory.

"education" in chocolate, and chocolate was among his favorite foods throughout his life. Indeed, his experience "testing" Cadbury's chocolate not only had an impact on his taste buds. It also helped him later in life when he was trying to come up with a story for his second children's novel, *Charlie and the Chocolate Factory*.[6]

> "'*There!*' cried Mr. Wonka, dancing up and down and pointing his gold-topped cane at the great brown river. 'It's *all* chocolate! Every drop of that river is hot melted chocolate of the finest quality. The *very finest* quality. There's enough chocolate in there to fill *every* bathtub in the *entire* country! *And* all the swimming pools as well! Isn't it *terrific*?'"[7]

Reading *Charlie and the Chocolate Factory*, you can practically smell the chocolate river running through Mr. Wonka's factory showroom—an amazing smell it would surely be! And listening to Dahl discuss the history of chocolate, you can actually believe he *would* fire all the history teachers in favor of teachers of chocolate—and those would be tough classes, to be sure. It might have been a subject most tempting to children, but Roald Dahl's imagination could entice children and adults alike.

Chapter 3

The Family from Norway

Born on September 13, 1916, Roald Dahl was the only son of Harald and Sofie Dahl, a Norwegian couple who lived in the southern part of Wales in Great Britain. The boy's parents gave him only one name, which in Norwegian is pronounced as "Row-ahl" without the sound of the final "d." It was an unusual name in Wales, perhaps, but it was also a reminder of the family's deep ties to their native Norway.

Roald Dahl described his father as a clever, hardworking man who loved beautiful things.[1] Harald Dahl had grown up in a family that was comfortable, but not wealthy, in a rather small town outside of Oslo, Norway. As a teenager, he fell off a roof and broke his left arm. Unfortunately, when the doctor came to help, he was drunk and thought Harald had dislocated his shoulder rather than broken his arm. In the process of trying to reset a shoulder which was not, in fact, dislocated, the doctor and his helpers made the situation significantly worse and young Harald Dahl's left arm had to be amputated at the elbow. Harald quickly learned how to do just about everything with his right hand alone. Roald later said that his father could tie a shoelace as quickly as anyone. Harald had created an "ingenious" utensil that served as both a fork and a knife. He carried it with him everywhere in a small leather case. According to family legend, the only inconvenience Harald ever faced was that he never figured out how to cut off the top of a boiled egg with only one hand.[2]

Harald and his brother Oscar were born about a year apart and they were very close. They were both very ambitious and clever and, though their father forbade it, they ran away from home as young men to seek their fortunes. The brothers were good friends, but they decided to go their separate ways. Oscar settled in France and became a wealthy businessman in the port town of La Rochelle. Harald, on the other hand, joined forces with another ambitious young Norwegian man named Aadnesen, and together they became shipbrokers in Cardiff, Wales. It was an important port in the 1890s, as it is today.

By that time, Harald had met and married a young French woman named Marie. By working hard and by being very clever, Dahl and Aadnesen were able to build their business and soon they each became quite wealthy. Harald and Marie moved to a beautiful house in Llandaff, a town outside of Cardiff, and they had two children, Ellen and Louis. Sadly, soon after the birth of their son Louis, Marie died, leaving Harald to grieve with two small children.

Though he was a successful businessman, Harald did not know many people in Wales, and after his grief had subsided, he decided to return to Norway on a holiday in hope of finding a new wife in his native land.[3] It was there in 1911 that he met Sofie Magdalene Hesselberg, a strikingly good-looking young woman. They met on a small coastal steamer and were engaged within a week and married soon after.[4]

Sofie's family was rather well-to-do. Her mother's family, the Wallaces, were the descendants of

> **The Wallaces were the descendants of the famous medieval Scottish hero Sir William Wallace.**

the famous medieval Scottish hero Sir William Wallace. Roald later found this tie to be of great interest.[5] Sofie, whose name was pronounced with three syllables, had read many books and like many people in her family, she was a great story-teller.

Roald Dahl and his mother were very close and

he loved her very much. Long after Sofie's death, Roald wrote, "She was undoubtedly the absolute primary influence on my own life. She had a crystal-clear intellect and a deep interest in almost everything under the sun, from horticulture to cooking to wine to literature to paintings to furniture to birds and dogs and other animals—in other words, in all the interesting and lovely things in the world."[6]

The Dahls were quite happy in Wales, but they were also very aware of their Norwegian roots. All of the children learned to speak Norwegian and all of them were christened in a Norwegian church located near the docks in Cardiff.[7] Every year, the family traveled to Norway to visit relatives and enjoy the beautiful countryside, especially Norway's dramatic cliff-lined waterways, or *fjords*.

Roald Dahl once described his parents as having been "deeply in love and blissfully happy"[8] and when the First World War was over, everything seemed right in the world. After a year of marriage, Sofie gave birth to a girl, Astri. Two years later, another daughter, Alfhild, was born. Roald was next in 1916 and Else followed the next year. In 1918, the family moved from the town of Llandaff to the small village of Radyr, about eight miles west of Cardiff. There they lived in "a mighty house with turrets on its roof and with majestic lawns and terraces all around it."[9]

Harald Dahl loved his children and wanted the best for them. He was a man who loved beautiful things and wanted to instill an appreciation of all things beautiful in the minds of his children. A romantic, Harald had a theory that this appreciation could begin even before the birth of a child, and thus, he developed the concept of the "glorious walk." At about six months into each pregnancy, Harald would announce that the "glorious walks" needed to begin. Harald would then take the pregnant Sofie out to beautiful places in the countryside where they would walk for an hour.[10] Harald and Sophie did this before the birth of all of their children. Whether it was a result of the walks or not, Roald in particular grew up to appreciate many beautiful things, including well-groomed gardens and fine paintings.

> **Dahl once described his parents as "deeply in love and blissfully happy."**

Sadly, the time of the glorious walks was cut short when tragedy struck the family. In February 1920, Astri Dahl, Harald and Sofie's eldest child, died suddenly of appendicitis at the age of seven. According to Roald, although Harald loved all his children, Astri was his favorite. Roald wrote that his father "adored [Astri] beyond measure and her sudden death left him literally speechless for days afterwards."[11] Overcome with grief, Harald caught pneumonia soon after Astri's death. Although penicillin had not yet been discovered, some people were able to survive pneumonia at that time—but they had to fight to overcome so very dangerous an illness. According to Roald, however, Harald had lost the will to live and he died a few months after Astri. The official cause of death was pneumonia, but many people attributed his death to a broken heart.

Sofie Dahl had lost her husband and eldest child in the span of just a few short months and she was several months pregnant with her fifth child. A stranger in a foreign land, Sofie now had to care for five children on her own: her own three surviving children, who were all under the age of five, and her husband's children from his first marriage, who were then in their teens. Sofie was a strong woman, however. Instead of returning home to Norway, Sofie decided to stay in Wales with the children. Harald had left behind a considerable financial legacy for his family, so money was not an immediate concern. She knew it was what her husband would have wanted her to do. After the birth of Asta in the fall of 1920, the family moved back to Llandaff to a smaller, more manageable house. It was there that Roald would go to school two years later at the age of six.

Chapter 4

Life at School

Llandaff is a medieval town near Cardiff in Wales with a beautiful cathedral and a green at its center. On the green stood the small Elmtree School, and this is where six-year-old Roald Dahl went to kindergarten.

Roald seems to have enjoyed his time there, but the greatest excitement he later remembered from that time was the trip back and forth to school each day. He and his eldest sister rode tricycles to school each day without any adults and they had a magnificent time. Dahl described it later in *Boy*: "No grown-ups came with us, and I can remember oh so vividly how the two of us used to go racing at enormous tricycle speeds down the middle of the road and then, most glorious of all, when we came to a corner, we would lean to one side and take it on two wheels."[1]

School was very important in the Dahl family. Roald Dahl later said that his father believed that England had become a world leader because of the education it offered its children. Harald Dahl always wanted his children to go to English schools.[2] Sofie Dahl was determined to honor her late husband's wishes. So young Roald began the process of preparing for a "proper" English school as soon as he was finished with kindergarten.

> **Young Roald began the process of preparing for a "proper" English school as soon as he was finished with kindergarten.**

Luckily for the Dahls, Llandaff was home to something other than just a beautiful cathedral and green. It also had a good preparatory school called the Llandaff Cathedral School, which was about a mile from the Dahls' house. This was the school that Roald attended from age six to nine. It was during this time that young Roald began to prepare for advanced schooling in England. It was also during this time that young Roald first began to cultivate two of his lifelong passions: writing and sweets.

As a young boy, Dahl was not the best of students, and he always had trouble with spelling. He had an active imagination, however, and an innate talent for storytelling, a talent he shared with other members of his family. In the Dahl family, this was extremely important, and the children were often regaled with stories by their mother and by their aunts whom they visited in Norway each summer.

Roald Dahl began his career as a writer at an early age. By age eight he had a diary, which he kept secret from his family. He guarded the diary by putting it in a waterproof box which he hid in a tree in the family's garden, knowing that his sisters would never climb the tree and discover his secret. Roald would climb the tree daily and from its lofty branches write in his diary, savoring the fresh air and his private treasure.[3]

It was at about this age that Roald and his friends began to frequent the sweetshop, owned by Mrs. Pratchett, which was located not far from their school. This was their favorite place in the world, though they did get into quite a bit of trouble one afternoon when they scared Mrs. Pratchett by putting the dead mouse in one of the candy jars.[4] After the "Great Mouse Plot," young Roald's mother decided that it was time her son began to fulfill his father's wish and she enrolled him at St. Peter's Preparatory School in Weston-super-Mare, Somerset. This boarding school was across the Bristol Channel from Cardiff in England. Roald was nine years old when he first went to St. Peter's in 1925, and he stayed there till the age of thirteen.

Dahl later described his time at St. Peter's as very difficult, but the stories that he told about the school may have been a bit exaggerated.[5] Before going to St. Peter's, Roald had never spent a night away from his family. No doubt it must have been very difficult to go away from home for the first time at such a young age, especially since Roald was very close to his sisters and mother.[6] During his first night away at school, Roald was very homesick and missed his family so much that he began to think about where they were in relationship to St. Peter's. Lying in bed, Roald thought about his family across the Bristol Channel and turned toward the window so he could be facing home. He later said that no matter which room he slept in at St. Peter's, he always did so facing his family and this helped to relieve his homesickness a little bit.[7]

As at the Llandaff Cathedral School, Roald was not a very good student at St. Peter's but he got along reasonably well with the other students. He was not particularly popular or unpopular, but he did have several good friends with whom he stayed close as he grew older.[8] He developed a passion for sports and was particularly good at cricket and swimming. Sports and games were to remain important throughout Dahl's life and he considered them an important part of a child's upbringing.

Students at St. Peter's were expected to write home to their families each week on Sunday mornings before going to church, and young Roald participated in this activity faithfully. Every week, Roald wrote to his mother, and he continued to do

The Llandaff Cathedral, where Roald Dahl attended
school between the ages of six and nine.

this long after he had left St. Peter's. In fact, Dahl wrote to his mother every week from the time he went to St. Peter's until she died in 1967, more than forty years later. After her death, Dahl discovered that his mother had saved every single one of the letters he had written to her. Without ever telling anyone, she had kept all of the original envelopes and stamps and had bundled them neatly with green tape. Dahl considered this to be a wonderful gift and greatly appreciated the fact that he could refer to his letters as he got older.

Back in Wales, the Dahl family prospered while Roald was at school, but eventually, Sofie decided to move the family to Bexley, in Kent, near London. When Roald finished his final term at St. Peter's, he was then sent to Repton, a well-known school about 140 miles north of London, near the town of Derby. Dahl was thirteen when he first went to Repton. His sisters all went to a girls' school called Roedean, in Sussex.[9]

> **Dahl was thirteen when he first went to Repton.**

In those days, Repton was not an easy school to go to, but not necessarily because the classes were hard or because the teachers were strict. Repton, like other boarding schools of that time, was a tough school in part because of the way the older boys ruled over the younger ones. Not only were teachers allowed to discipline students with beatings, but the older boys were also allowed to hit the younger ones if they misbehaved or did something out-of-line. The school had a strict hierarchy where prefects (older boys who organized house activities and study halls) had seemingly complete, and sometimes cruel, power. Though the adult Dahl occasionally exaggerated the extent of this cruelty, many of his contemporaries agreed that Repton could be a place of terror for its students.[10]

At Repton, Dahl was fortunate that he once again excelled at sports, and he even became the captain of the Fives team, a great honor at the school. Fives is a game similar to handball, but it has a different kind of court and a more complicated points system. Dahl played Eton-Fives while at Repton, which is played by four people, two on each side of the court.[11] In addition to Fives, Dahl also played squash, hockey, football (the American soccer), and cricket. He also did well in swimming. In his final year, Dahl even won the school boxing competition. Often, students who excelled at sports were made prefects, or "boazers" as the students called them, but Dahl was not made a prefect. He later wrote that this was just as well since he would have been a "rotten Boazer" because he would have refused to beat his fellow students.[12]

> **At Repton, Dahl was fortunate that he excelled at sports.**

It was at Repton that Dahl first became interested in photography. The art of photography required much more practice time in those days. Dahl took this hobby very seriously and honed his talents by spending many hours in a small darkroom set up at the back of the school. He continued to be an avid photographer throughout his life and even won several prizes for his photographic work as an adult.

Just before his final year at Repton, Dahl bought a used motorcycle, an Ariel 500cc. He hid it in a garage a few miles from the school. Every Sunday afternoon, the only time the students had free time, Dahl would put on a pair of goggles and a helmet and race around the countryside. Students at Repton were forbidden to own motorcycles and Dahl would have been punished severely if he had ever been caught by the headmaster or any of the school's teachers. Toward the end of his life, he looked back on that motorcycle with great fondness: "It was a wonderful big powerful machine and when I rode upon it, it gave me an amazing feeling of winged majesty and of independence that I had never known before. Wherever I wished to go, my mighty Ariel would take me."[13]

This was the beginning of Dahl's love of adventure, which would dominate his life for many years after leaving school in July 1933.

Chapter 5

Africa and Shell Oil

Roald Dahl always had a great thirst for adventure, even as a young man. When he was sixteen, Dahl went on his first vacation without his family. Instead of going with his mother and sisters to Norway as they did every August, that year Dahl chose to travel to France, where he planned to travel south to see the Mediterranean Sea. Aside from that, he had no plans and only twenty-four pounds in his pocket. In 1933 this was enough money for a two-week vacation. He ended up at St. Jean Cap Ferrat, a beach town where he had a wonderful time doing whatever he wanted from the time he got up in the morning until he went to sleep at night. He said, "It was my first taste of absolute freedom and my first glimpse of what it was going to be like to be a grown-up in a grown-up world."[1]

After finishing school at Repton, Dahl decided that he would rather travel than continue on to study at a university like Oxford or Cambridge, where many of his classmates were heading. Dahl decided that the best way to do this would be to apply to work for one of the large international corporations that could send him all over the world. With such pursuits in mind, he applied to Shell Oil Company during his final term of school.

Shell was a large company with offices and outposts all over the globe and with its own culture. In some ways, it had many of the same characteristics associated with the schools of the time. Like at Repton, at Shell there were many social rules and things employees were expected to do. While still in school, Dahl learned that Shell had accepted him, and he could not wait for the adventure to start in the autumn after school had ended.

Upon finishing school, Dahl decided to prepare for his Shell adventures by joining a group called The Public Schools' Exploring Society. He went with this group of adolescent boys on an exploration of the interior of Newfoundland that August. It was a challenging trip—the boys hiked all over the unmapped territory and they had to carry everything with them, including tents, pots and pans, food, and anything else they might need on the twenty-day march. Dahl recalled that his pack weighed more than one hundred pounds and he needed help just getting it on his back each morning![2] Although the boys did not discover gold or magic mountains like they had hoped at the start of their journey, they did learn how to survive many hardships. Dahl returned home excited, fit, and ready for his next journey.

In comparison with the trip to Newfoundland, the next few years were quite tame for Roald, though it was an important time for him nonetheless. After returning from his wilderness trek, Dahl became a Shell trainee in September 1934 at the age of eighteen. For the next few years, Dahl was a typical English businessman. Every day he took the train from Bexley, Kent, to London, wearing his hat and carrying his umbrella like all the other commuters. Every day he went to the Shell offices where he learned all there was to know about oil and the Shell Company. During this time, Dahl lived at home with his mother and sisters. In addition to going to work each day, he continued to practice his photography and golf or go to the racetrack with a few friends from school. Dahl enjoyed his time as a trainee, but he longed to travel abroad. When he was offered a post in Dar es Salaam in eastern Africa, he jumped at the chance.

> **Dahl enjoyed his time as a trainee, but he longed to travel abroad.**

It was the adventure that Dahl had been waiting for. Though it would send him far away from his beloved family, he could not wait to get started on the journey. His mother and sisters went to the docks to see him off. Despite the many dangers he might face in Africa, Dahl was very excited. He later wrote, "It was a tremendous thing in those days for a young man to be going off to Africa to work . . . I couldn't wait."[3]

Dahl set off on his journey on the SS *Mantola*. The trip took two weeks, with many ports of call between England and Mombassa, a town in what is now Kenya. From there he traveled on another boat, the *Dumra*, to Dar es Salaam, which is in the country now called Tanzania, but which was known as Tanganyika at the time. The trip from Mombassa to Dar es Salaam took only one day and one night. The next morning, Dahl woke up in the harbor of Dar es Salaam. In his second autobiography for children, *Going Solo*, Dahl recalled his first vision of the town that would be his home for the next few years. To him it seemed like a beautiful tropical paradise teeming with adventure—and nothing like London. He wrote, "The whole of that amazing tropical scene through the port-hole has been photographed on my mind ever since. To me it was all wonderful, beautiful and exciting. And so it remained for the rest of my time in Tanganyika. I loved it all. There were no furled umbrellas, no bowler hats, no sombre grey suits and I never once had to get on a train or a bus."[4] Though he missed his family, he did not miss his life as a London businessman, a life he never took up again.

While in Dar es Salaam, Dahl lived with two other young Englishmen and together they ran the Shell business in that part of Africa. The three young men managed the company in a territory four times the size of their native Great Britain. In doing so, they had a kind of power that put them on par with the colonial administrators and other officials in the area.[5]

> **"That amazing tropical scene through the port-hole has been photographed on my mind ever since."**
>
> **—Roald Dahl**

Dahl's job was to keep Shell customers supplied with lubricating oil or fuel oil for their machinery and factories. He was often required to go on long trips to reach these customers. Sometimes he was gone for a month or more, driving all around the region, seeing giraffes, elephants, hippos, and sometimes even a whole pride of lions. Dahl was not afraid of any of these animals, except for the snakes, which could be deadly killers. It was dangerous work sometimes, but he loved it.

In Dar es Salaam, Dahl and the other Shell employees lived in a big company house outside of town, on the cliffs overlooking the Indian Ocean.[6] There were several servants who also lived on the grounds of the house, including a cook the

Englishmen affectionately called Piggy because of the way the Swahili word for cook, *mpishi*, sounded. There was also a gardener named Salimu and a personal servant for each of the Shell employees. Dahl's servant was named Mdisho and he was a Mwanumwezi tribesman. The relationship between the two men was more than the relationship between master and servant—in many ways, Mdisho was Dahl's greatest friend in Africa. According to Dahl, Mdisho "was tall and graceful and soft-spoken, and his loyalty to me . . . was absolute. I hope, and I believe, that I was equally loyal to him."[7]

In order to communicate with Mdisho, the other servants, and other people from the region, Dahl and his colleagues had to learn Swahili. To do this, Dahl used a Swahili-English dictionary and grammar book and put in much hard work in the evenings after his Shell duties were completed for the day.[8] His Swahili improved so much that eventually he began to give reading and writing lessons to Mdisho, who had been illiterate. While teaching Mdisho how to read and write Swahili, he also taught him some English words, even though this was not considered proper at the time.[9] According to Dahl, Mdisho loved his lessons and was quick to learn, and this made both men very proud.

In addition to his work for Shell, Dahl continued to play a lot of sports while in Africa, though he often had to do so in 90-degree heat.[10] He sailed, swam, and played soccer, tennis, and, of course, one of his favorite games, golf. He later remembered having to watch out for cobras when playing golf in Dar es Salaam. He recalled that on one course in Kenya, players were allowed to lift their balls without penalty from the hoofprints left by a rhinoceros![11]

There were other activities for the Shell employees of course, including dinners and parties at the club for Europeans. But Dahl's social circle was relatively small. He knew his clients and some of the other Europeans in town, but did not have many close friends. While on his safaris to clients in the interior of the country, he often stayed with the British colonial district officers and their families, but these visits were infrequent. Indeed, Dahl often spent his free time writing to his family and listening to records, which he ordered from abroad. The lack of company, however, did not diminish the significance of this time in Africa for Dahl. He collected stories of terrifying snakes, a lion that tried to run off with the cook's wife, and much more—and he loved it.

Times were changing, however, and the Second World War was looming. Although the war would begin in Europe, its impact was felt in all corners of the globe, including eastern Africa. Dahl's time in Dar es Salaam was coming to an end, but a new adventure was just around the corner.

Chapter 6

Fighting in World War II

When Roald Dahl left Europe in the fall of 1938, he expected to work for Shell Oil in Africa for three years. War was coming, though, and everyone knew it, even Dahl and his fellow expatriates far away on the east coast of Africa. In his letters home in the early spring of 1939, Dahl begged his mother and sisters to leave their home in the suburbs of London in case there were bombings.[1] War was the unfortunate reality that was on the horizon, and he knew that no one would be able to escape it.

Things were even heating up in Dar es Salaam, though it was thousands of miles away from the battle lines being drawn in Europe. This was due to the fact that there were many Europeans living in the region, and many of the areas were controlled by European countries. Dar es Salaam, for example, had been under German control until being taken over by the British after the First World War. In addition, Italy's Mussolini was also trying to conquer another eastern African country called Abyssinia, which is now called Ethiopia.

During the spring and summer of 1939, Dahl and his fellow Englishmen in Africa prepared for war. In a letter written to his mother, Dahl told her that he had become a temporary army officer "with batons, belts and all sorts of secret instructions."[2] Although he had not had any military training except for some basic instruction at Repton, Dahl, along with the handful of other Englishmen in the area, was put in charge of a platoon of *Askaris*—soldiers in the King's African Rifles.

Dahl and his fellow Englishmen in Africa prepared for war.

Because Dar es Salaam once had been a German colony, there were hundreds of Germans still living in the area. The British army decided to put them in a prison camp as soon as war was declared. The prison camp was built but British officials felt certain that the German population would try to escape from the region rather than go to the camp. There was only one way to run and that would be along a coastal road going south. This was the road that Dahl was ordered to guard.

When war was declared, the Germans in Dar es
Salaam, many of them women and children,
attempted to flee, but Dahl and the Askaris troops
stopped them on the coastal road and they were
taken to the internment camp. Dahl was not happy
to have incarcerated his former neighbors, but he
did his duty.[3]

After war was declared, the call to arms sounded
around the globe to Englishmen living in all corners of the world. Heeding the call, Dahl told
the Shell Oil Company that he wanted to join the
British Royal Air Force, or the RAF. Recognizing
Dahl's patriotism, the Shell Company relieved him
of his duties immediately. Dahl quickly said good-
bye to Dar es Salaam and began the journey north
to Nairobi to begin his training.

As soon as he got to Nairobi, Dahl underwent
a medical examination. He was declared fit
for service, though his six-foot, six-inch height
was rather tall for a fighter pilot. There were
no height restrictions for pilots at the time,
so Dahl was given a uniform and the rank of
leading aircraftman, or LAC. As one of Dahl's
biographers, Jeremy Treglown, wrote, "With his
school cadet corps training, his individualism, and
his aptitude for games—particularly, his squash
player's reflexes—Dahl was a stereotypical fighter-
pilot recruit."[4] Along with his fellow trainees, who
nicknamed him "Lofty" because of his height,
Dahl spent the next six months learning how to
fly, fight, and navigate. He had a wonderful time,
aside from the fact that he did not have any

servants anymore, and he loved the training. He asked himself, "How many young men . . . were lucky enough to be allowed to go whizzing and soaring through the sky above a country as beautiful as Kenya?"[5]

The beauty of Kenya was a great contrast to Habbaniya in the Iraqi desert, the location of the camp where Dahl was sent to finish his fighter-pilot training. Here the young recruits really learned how to be fighter pilots. Aside from the flying, however, there was not much else to recommend Habbaniya and Dahl and his comrades could not wait to go into battle. Finally, with the heat blazing and the boredom rising, Dahl and the other trainees got their "wings": their training was complete and they were considered ready to go into battle. Dahl was promoted to the rank of pilot officer and became a fighter pilot. He was sent to an RAF station on the Suez Canal in eastern Egypt where, in mid-September 1940, he was assigned to 80 Squadron, which was then stationed in western Egypt near Libya.[6]

Unfortunately, it would actually be several months before anyone in 80 Squadron would ever meet Roald Dahl. On September 19, 1940, Dahl took off in a plane called a Gladiator to fly to meet his new squadron. He had never flown that kind of plane before. He was nervous but willing to give it a try, especially since his commanding officers had ordered him to deliver the plane to his new squadron. Dahl had to stop to refuel the plane twice and at the second landing, he was given directions that were not accurate.

Dahl did not know it but 80 Squadron had been forced to move its headquarters and landing fields because of heavy fighting. The group was no longer anywhere near the original location. Following the directions he was given, Dahl came to the place where the squadron was supposed to be only to find a desolate patch of desert. He flew around, desperately searching for his comrades, aware that he was close to enemy territory and wasting precious fuel.

When he was just about out of fuel, Dahl realized that he had to try to land the plane or else he would face an uncontrollable crash landing.

Miraculously, Dahl was able to escape the damaged plane before passing out.

Unfortunately, he had to land the plane in the desert, and when he did, he hit a boulder. In the crash, Dahl was thrown forward and smashed his head into the reflector-sight in the plane's cockpit, fracturing his skull and driving his nose into his face. Miraculously, Dahl was able to escape the damaged plane before passing out. This effort saved his life because the plane burst into flames a few minutes later. Soon after, a British patrol saw the fire and found Dahl, bleeding profusely with a face so bruised and swollen that he was blind for several weeks. The damage to his head, nose, and back was so serious that it was two months before he was able to get out of the hospital bed.[7]

Despite having to have surgery on his nose and suffering from terrible headaches, Dahl refused the offer to go to England because he was afraid that if he went home, he would not be allowed to fly again. Instead, Dahl stayed in a hospital in Alexandria, Egypt, for five months. After he was released in February 1941, he stayed in Alexandria to recuperate for another four weeks in the luxurious home of a family of English expatriates, the Peels. When he was finally able to join 80 Squadron, the war was being fought fiercely, and the British had suffered many losses.

After his month's leave at the Peels' home, Dahl reported back for duty to find that 80 Squadron was no longer in the Middle East. They had been fighting for some time in Greece, where they had to face both German and Italian forces. At this point, 80 Squadron was no longer flying Gladiator planes, the type that Dahl crashed in the desert. Now they were flying planes called Hurricanes, and Dahl did not know how to fly this kind of plane. After two brief days of training in Egypt, Dahl was sent on the four-and-a-half-hour trip to Greece. The cockpit of the plane was so tiny that the "lofty" Dahl cramped up during the ride and had to be lifted out of the cockpit by two strong men when he finally reached his destination.[8]

Things were not going well for the British and their allies in Greece in 1941. The British were seriously outnumbered and the rate of loss—of both men and planes—was staggering. Supplies were low, and the communication system was practically nonexistent. Dahl could not have come at a worse time, though he actually only stayed in Greece for about two weeks. This brief period, however, was probably the most dangerous time in his whole life.

It is difficult to determine what really happened during this terrible fortnight in Greece. After arriving in his Hurricane from Egypt, Dahl was thrown in with a small group of pilots in a plane he did not really know how to fly. Plus, he was forced to fight against an enemy force that was larger and much better equipped than the British.

> **Things were not going well for the British and their allies in Greece in 1941.**

Early in his stay in Greece, Dahl met a friendly young man named David Coke who gave him a few pointers about how to fight the German and Italian planes, but aside from these brief conversations, he had no previous combat experience.[9] Regardless, Dahl fought with courage and skill and he shot down several enemy planes in the battles, including a few in the infamous Battle of Athens in late April 1941.[10] Despite the valiant efforts of the RAF, it was a losing battle, and 80 Squadron was forced back across the Mediterranean to Alexandria after nearly all of their planes were destroyed.

After a brief respite in Alexandria, where Dahl and the handful of surviving pilots recuperated again at the Peels' home, 80 Squadron was on its way again, this time to Haifa. It was at this time that Dahl met a group of Jewish refugees who had fled Germany for Palestine. The group included

> **Dahl fought with courage and skill and he shot down several enemy planes.**

about fifty orphans and an older man who helped 80 Squadron by offering them an additional landing strip near Mt. Carmel, an offer which was a great service for the RAF. Unlike some of his fellow pilots, Dahl did not know about the Nazi persecution of the Jewish population in Europe because in the time preceding the war, he had been in Africa where news had been sporadic. This encounter in Haifa gave him a new perspective on the war.[11]

Unfortunately, soon after the squadron reached Haifa, Dahl began to suffer from splitting headaches that caused him to black out temporarily when flying at high altitudes. When Dahl told the doctor about this, the doctor realized that the headaches and blackouts were probably caused by the injuries Dahl had received upon crashing in the desert near Libya the year before. Given the dangers of blacking out while in the cockpit, it was determined that he should absolutely not fly anymore. This was unfortunate since Dahl loved to fly and felt it was his duty to his country to fight in the war. But Dahl recognized the gravity of his injuries and obeyed the order to return to England. The only consolation was that he would get to see his family. He had not seen them since leaving to work for Shell in 1938.

Dahl sent his family a telegram to tell them he was coming home, and he began the long and harrowing journey across the Mediterranean Sea and into the Atlantic Ocean by boat. When he finally arrived in England, however, he found that his family had not received his telegram and so no one was there to meet him. Dahl's mother and sisters had moved from Kent after their home was bombed, and they were living in a town called Grendon Underwood, which was about fifty miles from London. After some confusion, Dahl tracked down one of his sisters who was able to tell him where his mother was living. All of his family was thrilled that he was alive and home, and they were soon reunited.

Chapter 7

The War and the 1940s

Dahl had missed his family greatly while working in Africa and then fighting in the war, and the letters that passed between them were many. The mail was slow in those days due to the war, and, of course, letters are not a good substitute for loved ones far away. So Dahl was very happy to be reunited with his mother and sisters. He brought them gifts of limes and marmalades and silks from his travels.[1]

Dahl was promoted from pilot officer to flying officer upon being sent back to England. This was a relatively high rank. Even though he was not allowed to fly anymore, as an RAF officer he was often treated like a hero. Life in wartime England was difficult, though, and most of the other young men were away fighting the war, which was not going well then. Dahl had served his country honorably, but now that he was home, he did not know what to do with himself.

There were not many things to do in London at this time besides work related to the war, so Dahl lived a rather quiet life, especially compared to his adventures in Africa. Looking for something to do, Dahl used some of his savings to begin collecting art, a hobby that would last throughout his life. In beginning his collection, Dahl became friends with a painter named Matthew Smith, an older man whose sons had recently been killed in the war.[2] Smith eventually painted a portrait of Dahl, and he taught Dahl some of the finer points of art and art collecting.

> **Dahl lived a rather quiet life, especially compared to his adventures in Africa.**

In December 1941, the United States entered the war. By this point, Great Britain had been fighting virtually a lone battle for two years. There was a need for strong communication between the allies. Always a charming and gregarious young man, at a dinner party Dahl caught the attention of Harold Balfour, England's Undersecretary of Air.[3] Recognizing Dahl's social skills and his ability to make his way among all kinds of people, the Undersecretary arranged to have Dahl sent to Washington, D.C., to join the British Embassy there as an assistant air attaché.

It was Dahl's first visit to the United States. As

an RAF hero and a member of the British Embassy staff, he soon found himself mingling with all kinds of interesting people. He became friends with philosopher and political theorist Isaiah Berlin, future advertising giant David Ogilvy, and the wealthy Ivar Bryce, who introduced Dahl to Ian Fleming, the future author of the James Bond thrillers. The Embassy encouraged Dahl to get to know some of his American counterparts in addition to some of the more influential figures in Washington society. This proved easy for Dahl—he was a wonderful storyteller and dinner companion and he was handsome as well. One of the people he met at this time was Charles Marsh, a newspaper tycoon who had ties to the American government. Marsh liked the young pilot so much that he introduced him to many of his high-society friends. Marsh and Dahl would remain friends until Marsh's death in 1964.

Although Dahl's social life was in full swing, the war was not going well. It was a time of great struggle for the Allies, and newspapers and magazines were on the lookout for stories that would boost their readers' morale—even if the stories needed to be stretched a bit to do so. A handsome bachelor who was popular on the scene in Washington, Dahl was the perfect candidate for such a morale-boosting story, and so the *Saturday Evening Post* sent the famous novelist C.S. Forester to interview him. Dahl and Forester had such fun when they met for lunch, however, that they never got around to conducting the interview.

To help his new friend, Dahl offered to write up some notes about his experiences. Forester apparently liked Dahl's reminiscences so much that he sent the notes to the *Saturday Evening Post* under Dahl's name. Eventually the story was printed as an anonymous article called "Shot Down Over Libya," in reference to a crash which

> **To help his new friend, Dahl offered to write up some notes about his experiences.**

was caused by gunfire from Italian fighters. Dahl's crash in the desert in 1940 had not been caused by enemy fire, which he later described in *Going Solo*, but it is unclear what he was responsible for writing in the *Post* story. It was quite common during the war for newspapers and magazines to spin tales a bit to boost morale. In any case, "Shot Down Over Libya" was well received. So was Roald Dahl the writer when it became known that he was author of the story.

During his time in wartime Washington, Dahl got to know just about everyone. He was invited to the White House, met movie starlets and writers, and was an active member of British intelligence in the United States. His bravado was extreme but not unusual or unwelcomed, for the most part. Word of the handsome British story-teller/war hero eventually reached executives in

Hollywood, including one of the biggest players in American cinema at the time—Walt Disney.

After the success of "Shot Down Over Libya," Dahl decided to try his hand at writing more seriously. He began to work on a story called "Gremlin Lore" which combined some of his love of Norwegian fairy tales with the myths told by RAF fighters in the war. In these myths, gremlins were small elves who caused problems and breakdowns on RAF planes. For example, it was the gremlins' fault if something broke, not human error. Among the superstitious fighters, gremlins were common features in conversations, but it was Dahl who brought them into the mainstream.[4]

Disney proposed making a feature film out of the story, and Dahl went back and forth to California several times to discuss the movie. Disney published some news about the possible film, which was much discussed among the members of the film industry and among RAF fighter pilots, many of whom claimed the gremlins as their own creations.[5] In the end, Disney did not make a feature film out of the story, but in 1943 did publish a book called *The Gremlins (A Royal Air Force Story by Flight Lieutenant Roald Dahl)*. It was Dahl's first book and the beginning of a long and sometimes controversial career as a writer.

Chapter 8

Marriage and Family

After the war ended in 1945, Dahl decided to be a writer. Rather than return to his old job at Shell, Dahl returned to his mother's home and sat down to work. For the next few years, that was his life— he wrote, followed dog racing and spent time with his family. By this time, the Dahl family had moved to Great Missenden, where the remaining Dahl family still lives today. Occasionally, Dahl would travel back and forth to the United States to visit the friends he had made there during the war, especially his old friend Charles Marsh. During this time, he wrote several short stories for adults. They included the ones in the book *Over to You*, a collection of war stories for adults which was published in 1946.

Over to You received some good reviews but

Dahl was not an instant success in England. In the United States, however, he was better received—as both a writer and a man-about-town. Eventually, he moved to New York, where he was considered "*The New Yorker*'s odd English writer, every season's bachelor-of-the-year."[1] It was a grand time for Dahl, who hobnobbed with the social elite and who was invited to dinners with literary giants. It was at one such dinner that he met the famous actress Patricia Neal.

Dahl was the "odd English writer, every season's bachelor-of-the-year."

Though she then moved in high society circles, Patricia Neal had more humble beginnings. She was born in Kentucky, the daughter of the manager of the town's coal mine. She had an older sister named Margaret Ann and a younger brother, William Petrey, who was called Pete. Pat had begun to act in Knoxville, Tennessee, where her family had moved when she was three. She went to Northwestern University for a year. Near the end of her first year of college, her beloved father died, and afterwards she moved to New York to be an actress.

Her first major Broadway role was in Lillian Hellman's *Another Part of the Forest* in 1946. It was a challenging play, but Neal got rave reviews for her performance. Soon she was invited to

Hollywood, where she starred in films with Ronald Reagan and Gary Cooper. Her biggest early film role was in *The Fountainhead* opposite Cooper. By 1952, however, she had decided to take a break from Hollywood, and so she came back to New York. When she met Dahl, she was about to star in another Hellman play, *The Children's Hour*.

Dahl had met the playwright Hellman during his time in the United States during the war, and like other people he recognized that she was a fascinating and powerful woman. At one of her famous dinner parties, she managed to seat Dahl next to the beautiful Neal—perhaps trying to play matchmaker or perhaps just trying to create interesting conversation at her table.

Theirs was not an auspicious first meeting but it was a memorable dinner for both Dahl and Neal. As she described it in her autobiography, *As I Am*, "I was absolutely sure that Mr. Dahl would spend the whole supper trying to charm me. I sat down and waited. But he began a conversation with Leonard Bernstein, seated across the table, that continued throughout the meal. Never once during the entire evening did he look my way. I tried to join the conversation but he totally ignored me. I was infuriated and tried to pretend his rudeness did not bother me in the least, but by the end of the evening I had quite made up my mind that I loathed Roald Dahl."[2]

Dahl's version of the story was similar and he did not try to pretend otherwise: "I behaved badly, I supposed. I was getting into one of those arguments with Lennie Bernstein, and there was no backing off from it. Pat thought I was rude and decided I was 'someone not to know,' as she says."[3]

Dahl asked Hellman for Neal's phone number, however, and he called her the next day. At first the beautiful young actress refused to see him, but eventually he convinced her to go out to dinner with him and that was the beginning of their long relationship. They were married in New York on July 2, 1953. It was a small wedding for just a few friends—the couple's families had difficulty traveling to New York, so plans were made to visit them later instead. At the end of their honeymoon in Europe, the newlyweds visited the Dahls in Great Missenden, England, and then they visited the Neals at Christmastime. Upon their return to New York, the couple moved into a new apartment near Central Park.

The Dahls' first child was born on April 20, 1955. The baby girl was named Olivia after a character in Shakespeare's *Twelfth Night*, which Neal had played at Northwestern.[4] Within a few months of her birth, the new family began to travel back and forth to Great Missenden, England, to visit with the Dahls. It was a busy time. By the time Olivia was three months old, Pat was back on Broadway in *A Roomful of Roses* and then in *Cat on a Hot Tin Roof*, which was directed by the famous Elia Kazan. Soon after that, Pat filmed the movie *A Face in the Crowd*.

Pat's career was going well and the new family seemed happy. Pat was soon pregnant again and

Roald Dahl and Patricia Neal are photographed outside of Trinity Church Chapel in New York on July 2, 1953, shortly after they were wed.

she continued to perform in the United States while Dahl began to set up their residence near his family in Great Missenden with baby Olivia. Pat came back to England in order to have their second child, a girl who was called Tessa, in April 1957.

During this time, Roald had spent a lot of time restoring their English home, which was originally called Little Whitfield. He turned an old gypsy caravan which sat on the property into a play house for the children, including his sisters' children who lived nearby. Eventually, the family renamed the property "Gypsy House" in honor of the beloved caravan.

While working on the house, Dahl also set up a small hut in which to write. This writing hut was where he spent much of his time when at the house in Great Missenden. Not only was it where he did most of his writing and spent much of his time, but it was also a place that housed many items of great personal value to him.

The writing hut was small and full of memorabilia from Dahl's life. A fellow writer once said, "The room reminded me of an aeroplane cockpit. This was his creative space capsule inside which his imagination blossomed with wild, mischievous ideas."[5] By the time Dahl died, the hut was a virtual treasure trove of his life, and all manner of trinkets and prizes could be found there, including a ball made out of chocolate bar wrappings which Dahl began when he first worked at Shell Oil after graduation from Repton, his father's silver and tortoiseshell paper knife, gifts sent to him by fans over the years, and one of his own hip bones which had been removed during an operation later in life.[6]

Dahl was determined to make his living as a writer of short stories and novels for adults. Once he got settled in the family's new home in England, Dahl began to set a schedule of writing which he would adhere to for much of his life. Typically, he would get up in the morning and respond to any mail he might have before filling up a thermos of coffee and heading out to the hut at around 10:30 A.M. He would spend the morning writing and then take a break for lunch. After reading for a little while in the early afternoon, Dahl would return to the hut for another few hours of writing.[7]

Although the family was setting up a home in Great Missenden, they were still going back and

> **Here was an audience for his storytelling—something both he and the children loved.**

forth to New York regularly for Pat's acting. They also went to Norway in the summer on the Dahls' annual holiday to visit relatives. In the summer of 1960, the Dahls' only son, Theo, was born in New York, and the family went back to England for a few months. Now the older children were growing out of babyhood and Dahl was in his element. Here was an audience for his storytelling— something both he and the children loved. A new career was about to begin.

It was about this time that Dahl began to tell one particular story as a way of entertaining his daughters Olivia and Tessa. After seeing the girls' reaction, he decided that he should write the story down and submit it to his editors, who were surprised to receive a children's story from this writer of adult fiction.

In the story, which was eventually called *James and the Giant Peach*, James is a young boy who is forced to live with his horrible Aunt Sponge and Aunt Spiker after his lovely and wonderful parents died in an accident. Aunt Sponge and Aunt Spiker lived in an old house on the top of a very tall hill from which you could see the ocean. They were very cruel to James and never let him play or see other children.

One day, when he was feeling particularly sad, James was sitting along in a quiet corner of the garden when he met a very odd stranger. This grizzly old man gave James a bag full of small green, glowing, magic things which he said would make James marvelously happy if he drank them in one fell swoop:

> ". . . you must quickly drink it all down, the whole jugful, in one gulp. And then, my dear, you will feel it churning and boiling in your mouth, and immediately after that, *marvelous* things will start happening to you—*fabulous*, *unbelievable* things . . . And don't let those green things in there get away

Roald Dahl and Patricia Neal with their children, Theo and Tessa.

from you either! Because if they do escape, then they will be working their magic upon somebody else instead of upon *you!* . . . *Whoever they meet first, be it bug, insect, animal, or tree, that will be the one who gets the full power of their magic!*"[8]

Unfortunately for James, or so it seemed at first, he accidentally dropped the bag full of shimmering green things, and they quickly burrowed underground around the old dried-up peach tree in Aunt Sponge and Aunt Spiker's garden. Almost immediately, the tree, which had never had any peaches on it, began to sprout a beautiful peach which grew so big that it was quickly the size of a small house. Soon, James found a hole near the base of the peach which led to a tunnel that ended

---

Pat's career was going well and the new family seemed happy.

---

in a large room inside the giant peach pit. If that were not surprising enough, inside the pit was a group of the most extraordinary creatures James had ever seen—giant insects as large as the largest dog he had ever met who welcomed him as one of their own happy crew. After cutting the peach's stem from the tree, James and the insects rolled down the hill away from Aunt Sponge and Aunt Spiker's nasty little house. They rolled and rolled and rushed and pounded, streaming through the countryside in the beautiful giant peach—and this was only the beginning of the adventure.

Dahl gave *James and the Giant Peach* to his editor, Alfred Knopf. In turn, Knopf showed it to the company's editor of children's books, Virginie Fowler, who loved the story and prepared it for publication.[9] Almost immediately, Dahl began work on another story which he had begun to tell his children, *Charlie and the Chocolate Factory*. This would become one of his most famous works. The year was 1960 and everything was going well for the Dahl family. The children—Olivia, Tessa, and Theo—were happy and healthy, and their parents' careers were becoming more and more successful. Unfortunately, this happiness would be short-lived. Tragedy was looming.

Chapter 9

A Decade of Tragedy

In the early 1960s, the Dahl family regularly crossed back and forth across the Atlantic Ocean, and the travels were exciting for the young family. With Pat's career in theater and television, New York was a natural place for their home in the United States, and with Roald's family so close, Great Missenden was a happy place for them in England.

In 1960, the family returned to New York so Pat could film *Breakfast at Tiffany's* with Audrey Hepburn and George Peppard. On December 5, Pat was out shopping near the family's apartment on the Upper East Side, and Roald was writing in his studio, a separate apartment in the same building. The family's nanny had taken Tessa and Theo with her for a walk to pick Olivia up from her school, which was two blocks away. Tessa was only three years old, and Theo, only four months, was in a baby carriage. After waiting for a light to change, the nanny took Tessa's hand and began to push the carriage in a crosswalk at a busy intersection. Just then, a taxicab barreled through the intersection, tearing the carriage right out of the hands of the young nanny. The carriage, with the baby inside, was thrown forty feet in the air and hit the side of a bus before coming to a stop. The nanny and Tessa were left standing on the sidewalk, stunned.

Within minutes, police and emergency personnel were there and the baby was rushed to Lenox Hill Hospital just a few blocks away. Nearby, Pat heard the sirens, but she did not find out what had happened until she went home and found the phone ringing.[1]

Theo was badly hurt. When the carriage hit the bus, it had collapsed on his head, and he was in very serious condition. After a few frantic days in the eastside hospital, Roald and Pat decided they wanted to move the baby to another hospital. Harvey Orkin, Pat's agent and friend, drove the terrified parents and their child across the city in the snow to Columbia Presbyterian Hospital. That was where the Dahl children's regular pediatrician practiced. Although they felt more comfortable there, it was still a frightening time since no one knew whether Theo would survive—and if he did, whether he would be severely brain damaged. This was a very real concern because one of his injuries required that doctors insert a shunt into his head.

This is a tube with a valve to drain excess fluid. This was a relatively new procedure and had serious side effects—the valve clogged regularly which caused the baby to suffer from high fevers and to go temporarily blind. Miraculously, doctors determined that Theo Dahl would live and after about a month, Roald and Pat took him home. That spring, the family moved back to England and tried to regain a sense of calm.

Later Roald said, "The only resistance was mine about going back to New York [in early 1960]. Gentle resistance, mind you—complaining a bit. But up until Theo's accident, New York was as much our headquarters as Great Missenden. Afterward, though, we didn't want to be there any more. The accident really cooked New York."[2]

> **"The accident really cooked New York."**
>
> **—Roald Dahl**

After returning to England, Roald continued to worry about Theo, especially since the baby had to undergo dangerous surgery frequently because the valve in the brain shunt kept clogging. Soon after returning to England, Roald began to work with Theo's new doctor, Kenneth Till, and an acquaintance, Stanley Wade, to create a new valve that would not clog as easily. The new valve, the Wade-Dahl-Till Valve was patented and by June 1962, it was being used on children in England successfully.[3] As it turned out, Theo never needed to use the valve which his father had helped to invent because he unexpectedly got better. The doctors were able to remove the shunt and its old clogging valve and they did not need to replace it. For a while, things seemed to be looking up for the Dahl family—Roald was even able to finish a new draft of *Charlie and the Chocolate Factory*, which he dedicated to Theo.

Charlie and the Chocolate Factory is one of the most beloved of all children's stories and one of Dahl's most famous novels. The book tells the tale of Charlie Bucket, a young boy from a poor family who lived in a small house on the outskirts of a large city. Charlie's family was so poor that their home was often freezing in the winter and all four of Charlie's old grandparents slept in the one large bed in the main room of their small house. The four old grandparents were so old and so tired that they never got out of bed, and Charlie and his parents had to sleep on a mattress in the other room. The Buckets never had much to eat and though they did not starve, their stomachs were always grumbling. Charlie's stomach especially grumbled for chocolate, the "one thing he longed for more than anything else."[4] What made this grumbling worse was the fact that the Buckets' small house stood right in sight of a huge chocolate factory owned by Mr. Willy Wonka.

Mr. Wonka was "the most *amazing*, the most *fantastic*, the most *extraordinary* chocolate maker the world has ever seen!"[5] And his factory was just as marvelous. After closing the factory to outside visitors for many months, Mr. Wonka announced a contest that would allow five lucky children the chance to visit his factory and have as much chocolate as they wanted for the rest of their lives. The winners would be those children who found Golden Tickets hidden inside bars of Wonka's chocolate.

The five fortunate children were Augustus Gloop, Veruca Salt, Violet Beauregarde, Mike Teavee, and, the hero, Charlie Bucket. After they entered the factory, the children, except Charlie, behaved badly and one by one they experienced various "adventures" involving sweets, chocolate rivers, candy-making machines, squirrels, and the mysterious Oompa-Loompas, the tiny workers in Mr. Wonka's factory.

The Dahls had returned to England hoping for happier times. Though *Charlie and the Chocolate Factory* was progressing well, these happy times were also short-lived. In the fall of 1962, measles broke out at Olivia Dahl's school. Measles was not considered particularly dangerous at the time, and few children received inoculations against it as they do today. On rare occasions, children suffered complications, but more often, they contracted the disease and recovered easily. When the Dahls learned of the outbreak at their daughter's school, they were concerned, however, because of Theo—though he was doing better, they were afraid that he would not fare well if he caught the disease. Roald's older sister Ellen was married to a prestigious doctor, and though he could not get enough measles vaccine for all the children, he helped Roald and Pat get some for Theo. No one was particularly concerned about Olivia and Tessa. Getting the measles was almost like a right of passage, and the adults thought it might be just as well if they got it over with at a young age.

A few days after Theo's inoculation, Olivia became ill. At first no one worried too much because she regularly came down with minor colds and coughs. After putting her into a separate room from the other children, Pat and Roald tried to cheer her up by calling her their "fantastically polka-dotted daughter."[6]

The Dahls had returned to England hoping for happier times.

Soon Olivia seemed to be very ill, much more so than her worried parents expected. She was listless and would not even play when her father made her little animals out of pipe cleaners.[7] The family doctor was not concerned, though, and told Pat and Roald not to worry. Unfortunately, no one knew that Olivia actually had a very serious and rare form of measles called measles encephalitis. A few days later, on November 17, 1962, Olivia slipped into a coma and, within hours, she died. She was only seven, the same age as Roald's older sister Astri when she died of appendicitis. The family was devastated, especially Roald who, according to Pat, "all but lost his mind after Olivia died."[8]

The Dahl family greatly mourned Olivia's death. But Pat and Roald knew that they had to provide for their other children. Slowly, they went back to work. Pat took a few jobs working in television as Roald tried to escape from a writer's block induced by the tragedies that his children had suffered. It was at about this time that Pat was offered a role in a new Hollywood film starring Paul Newman. The movie was called *Hud* and although Pat had to go back to the United States to film the movie, she was able to return to visit the family when the movie production was between locations.

Hud premiered in the late spring of 1963, and Pat received rave reviews for her portrayal of Alma, a relatively small but important role in the film. She was even nominated for an Academy Award. And, to add to this happiness, she was pregnant again. The Academy Awards ceremony was in April 1964. Because Pat was so far along in her pregnancy, the Dahls stayed in England, not thinking that Pat would actually win the Oscar. Because of the time difference between England and Los Angeles, they were asleep during the ceremony. They were awakened in the middle of the night by a phone call from an excited friend, telling them that Pat had indeed won the Academy Award![9] Even better, Pat delivered a healthy baby girl, Ophelia Magdalena Dahl, less than a month later.

Soon, the entire family was back in the United States for another film for Pat. In the fall of 1964,

Charlie and the Chocolate Factory was released to great acclaim in the United States. By the New Year, the family was settled into a friend's home in Los Angeles as Pat began preparations for a film called *Seven Women*. Then Roald and Pat discovered that she was pregnant again. At this time, Roald was beginning to work on a screenplay called *O Death, Where Is Thy Sting-a-ling-a-ling?*, which was to be directed by Robert Altman but

> ## In the fall of 1964, *Charlie and the Chocolate Factory* was released to great acclaim.

was never produced. Otherwise things seemed to be going well, but unfortunately, this brief period of happiness was not to last either.

One evening, just a few days after the shooting of her new film had begun, Pat was helping Tessa, then almost eight, in the bath. Suddenly she felt a pain in her head. As Tessa looked on in fear, Pat made her way back into the bedroom to Roald who knew immediately that something was very wrong. Within minutes, Pat was unconscious and an ambulance was on its way. Pat had suffered an aneurysm, a kind of a stroke, and before the night was over, she suffered two more. It was a terrible blow to her and her family who had already experienced so much hardship in such a short amount of time.

No one knew if Pat was going to live, and Roald and the children were very worried. After very intricate surgery, Pat was in the hospital for about a month, and when she returned home, the children found that their mother could hardly walk or talk—her words were often jumbled and she struggled to make sense. She was still pregnant, but no one knew if the baby would be all right. Doctors were not optimistic about her recovery, but Roald was convinced that she would be back to work within a year.[10]

The next few years were very difficult as Pat struggled to regain her speech, her ability to walk, and her independence. Fortunately, the new baby, Lucy Neal Dahl, was born healthy on August 4, 1965, just five months after Pat's stroke. At that point, Pat could walk with just a slight limp, but she still could not speak well. Roald set up a strict system of exercises to help her improve, and he was still convinced that she would make a full recovery.

Roald's recuperation plan involved a group of helpers who worked with Pat every day on a series of exercises that were designed to teach her how to talk, read, and write again. After Lucy was born, a woman named Valerie Eaton Griffith became Pat's main helper, and Roald was able to spend more time trying to support the family with his writing.[11]

In need of money to support his family, which now consisted of four young children, Roald decided to accept an offer to return to film writing.

Roald Dahl and Patricia Neal with their children, Tessa, Ophelia, and Theo (left to right) in 1965.

Roald agreed to write the screenplay for a very big project—a new James Bond movie called *You Only Live Twice*, which was released in June 1967. The movie was a great success and helped the family financially during Pat's recovery.

Although *You Only Live Twice* was a smash at the box office and Roald was compensated well for his work, things were still difficult at home. Pat's recovery was going slower than Roald had hoped, and he pushed her very hard. To make matters worse, soon after the release of *You Only Live Twice*, Roald had to have an operation on his spine. He suffered severe pains in his back and neck, complications from the injuries he received

---

Roald was convinced that she [Pat] would be back to work within a year.

---

in World War II. While he was in the hospital, Roald's 82-year-old mother, Sofie, called to see how he was. Worried about her only son, she did not mentioned that she herself was gravely ill and she passed away a few days later on November 17, the fifth anniversary of Olivia Dahl's death.

Despite the pain in his back and the sorrow from his mother's death, Roald continued to work during this time. After *You Only Live Twice*, Dahl began work on another movie, *Chitty Chitty Bang*

Roald Dahl escorts his wife, Patricia Neal, to a movie premiere in December 1968.

Bang, which was cowritten by Kenneth Hughes, the director of the movie. This movie was also a box-office hit but it was a challenge for Dahl, who had several disagreements with the director. It was at about this time that talks began about a movie version of *Charlie and the Chocolate Factory*.

The movie, *Willy Wonka and the Chocolate Factory*, as it was renamed, began production in 1970. Dahl had originally written a screenplay for the movie, which was to be directed by Mel Stuart. After several drafts, Stuart and the production team determined that "Dahl had created a script that was, in many ways, a replica of his original novel. Unfortunately, many of the developments that worked so well in his children's story could not be transferred directly to the screen."[12]

Gene Wilder as Willy Wonka, along with his Oompa-Loompas, in a publicity photo for the 1971 film *Willy Wonka and the Chocolate Factory*.

Dahl agreed to the changes the producers wanted and went back to work. In the meantime, the producers hired a young man named David Seltzer to work on the script. When Dahl heard about this, he was upset and urgently invited Stuart to his home. According to Stuart, upon arriving at Great Missenden, he gave Dahl the Seltzer-revised script, which Dahl read immediately while Stuart waited. After reading the new script, Dahl agreed to all the changes and from then on, the movie was more or less out of his hands.

Ultimately, *Willy Wonka and the Chocolate Factory*, which starred the emerging actor Gene Wilder, was a great success when it came out in 1971, and it increased the sale of Dahl's books throughout the world. Roald was happy about the success of his work but frustrated by working in the film world. *Willy Wonka and the Chocolate Factory* was his last attempt at screenwriting. It was not the last time his work would be made into a movie, however, and Roald's fame as a children's writer continued to increase. Things were looking brighter than they had in a long time.

A few weeks after Roald's mother's death, in an interview with a writer from *LIFE* magazine who was writing a book about the Dahls, Pat said, "Do you know that it's seven years since bad things started happening to us? On December 5, it will be seven years since Theo was hit. If it's a seven-year curse, it better stop now, boy. These bad things better stop happening to us."[13]

Thankfully, it did indeed seem as if the tragedies were over.

Chapter 10

A Writer's Empire and the End of an Era

After many challenging months, Pat was improving, albeit slowly. Roald pushed her in her recovery, which occasionally caused them to argue. In the end, Pat was grateful to him for getting her there—even if it had been a very tough road.

Later in life, when writing about her first public appearance after her stroke—a speech at a charity for brain-injured children—Pat said, "Before I realized it, I had finished the speech. People stood and wept and cheered. I knew then that my life had been given back to me for something more than I had imagined. Mind you, I had no idea what that could possibly be. But I knew at that moment that Roald the slave driver . . . with his relentless scourge, Roald the Rotten, as I had called him more than once, had thrown me back into the deep water. Where I belonged."[1] Once again, however, the calm was relatively short-lived.

Pat began to act again, and in the early 1970s, she agreed to do a commercial for Maxim Coffee. In the commercials, she referred to her husband Roald and described how both of them loved the coffee, which they had tested for several months before shooting the commercials. Roald and Pat really did like the coffee and they thought the commercials were fun. The production staff was courteous and professional, and the Dahls liked all of them, especially an attractive woman named Felicity Crosland who was a stylist for the advertising company.

Felicity, whose nickname was Liccy, helped provide Pat with dresses for the commercials and she always seemed to have the best taste. She and Pat got along quite well, and soon Liccy was a regular guest at the Dahls' house in Great Missenden.[2]

At the time, Liccy was in her mid-thirties and recently divorced. She was born in Llandaff, Wales, not far from where Roald had been born, and she had a very interesting heritage. One of her ancestors had been married to Sir Walter Raleigh and had been imprisoned with him in the Tower of London![3] She also had three daughters, whose names were Neisha, Charlotte, and Lorina, and she would often bring them when she went to visit the Dahls. Soon, the families went on vacations together and spent many holidays in each others' company. At first no one realized it—least of all Pat—but Roald and Liccy soon fell in love. When Pat found out, she was very upset, and Pat and Roald's marriage began to deteriorate.[4]

Despite the changes happening in his family life, Dahl was very busy writing at this time. One of his most popular books was *Danny, the Champion of the World*, which was published in 1975 and which he dedicated to "the whole family, Pat, Tessa, Theo, Ophelia, Lucy."[5]

Danny tells the story of a young boy who lives with his father in a gypsy caravan on the site of a gas station on the outskirts of a town. The gypsy caravan was modeled after the one that stood on the land of the Dahls' home in Great Missenden, after which the family had renamed their home in 1963.[6]

In the story, the boy's mother had passed away when he was just an infant, and Danny and his father had a very close relationship, perhaps the kind of relationship that Roald hoped he could have had with his own father—and one he tried to have with his own children. The novel is about Danny's adventures with his father, including one in which Danny came up with such a grand plan that his father called him "the champion of the world!"[7]

At the end of the novel, Dahl wrote a message to children and their parents: "When **you** grow up and have children of your own, do **please** remember something **important**. A STODGY parent is no fun at all! What a child wants—and DESERVES—is a parent who is sparky!"[8]

In 1975, Dahl began to collaborate with the illustrator Quentin Blake, with whom he would work for the rest of his life. A quiet man, Blake was a professor at the Royal College of Art and he was already quite well known as an illustrator by this time.

The pair's first collaboration, *The Enormous Crocodile*, was a great success and soon it was obvious that Blake's drawings and Dahl's stories complimented each other well. Later in life, Dahl wrote, "I and most of my family are privileged to know [Quentin Blake] well and everyone adores him . . . It is the faces and the bodies he draws that are remembered by children all over the world."[9]

> **"A STODGY parent is no fun at all!"**
>
> **—Roald Dahl**

Blake enjoyed working with Dahl as well. He later said, "What was so nice about Roald was that he actually wanted the pictures—he didn't like it if there weren't enough. Not all authors are like that."[10]

The first full-length novel that Blake and Dahl worked on together was *The BFG*, which was published in 1982. One of Dahl's most beloved stories, *The BFG* tells the tale of a young orphan girl named Sophie. One night, while lying in bed in her dormitory, Sophie was snatched away by a giant, the BFG in fact, whose initials stood for "Big Friendly Giant."

While most giants liked to eat small children, the BFG did not and instead his diet consisted only of "snozzcumbers." This disgusting "extremely icky-poo vegetable" was the only thing around for a giant to eat if he did not like to eat small children, and so this was all that was on the BFG's menu.[11] The BFG had stolen young Sophie from her bed because she had seen him while he was delivering dreams to the children in her town, but they got along quite well once they learned how to understand each other's way of speaking. Together, Sophie and the BFG devised a plan to stop the other giants from snatching and then eating children, and in the course of their adventures, they even got to meet the Queen of England!

The collaboration between Dahl and Blake was very significant in the creation of *The BFG*. For instance, after seeing some of Blake's drawings of the BFG, Dahl decided to change what the giant wore because it did not look right in the drawings. Eventually, the giant ended up wearing sandals rather than knee-high boots because Dahl and Blake liked the drawing better that way.[12] After searching for many years to find an illustrator who really understood him, Dahl had finally found a partner in Quentin Blake.

Other relationships were changing for Dahl at this time as well, however. In 1983, Pat and Roald divorced after thirty years of marriage. Later that year, Liccy and Roald were married and began to live together in the Dahl home in Great Missenden. With the success of *The BFG* and his other novels for children, Dahl was becoming even more famous. Beginning in 1983, he entered into an extremely productive time in his life as a writer.

In 1983, *The Witches* was published and it quickly became one of Dahl's most popular books. Inspired by the Norwegian folklore of Dahl's childhood, *The Witches* tells the story of a young boy who lived with his Norwegian grandmother. Early in the novel, the narrator explains, "The

> **Beginning in 1983, he entered into an extremely productive time in his life as a writer.**

Norwegians know all about witches, for Norway, with its black forests and icy mountains, is where the first witches came from."[13] One day, while on holiday with his grandmother by the seaside, the hero discovered that all of the witches of England were at their hotel having their Annual Meeting, and he and his grandmother had to devise a brilliant plan in order to protect the children of the world.[14]

After *The Witches* was published to great acclaim, Dahl continued to work productively. With the publication of the short picture book *The Giraffe and the Pelly and Me* in 1984, Dahl decided that he wanted to tell his life story in his own words. He did so in two volumes. The first book, *Boy*, was published in 1984, and the second, *Going Solo*, came out in 1986. *Boy* tells the story of Dahl's early childhood and ends with his completion of school and his early days at the Shell Oil Company. *Going Solo* begins with Dahl's journey to Africa with Shell and describes his adventures in World War II. There were some people who challenged Dahl's version of events in these books, but both are important illustrations of how Dahl saw himself and the image that he wanted to present to the world.

After these two autobiographical works were completed, Dahl began to work on what would be his last full-length novel, *Matilda*, which was published in 1988. In this story, Matilda is a smart, friendly young girl whose parents were particularly cruel. The Wormwoods, for that was their name, "looked upon Matilda in particular as nothing more than a scab. A scab is something you have to put up with until the time comes when you can pick it off and flick it away. Mr. and Mrs. Wormwood looked forward enormously to the time when they could pick their little daughter off and flick her away, preferably into the next county or even further than that."[15]

> **Dahl's last full-length novel, *Matilda*, was published in 1988.**

Matilda, however, was brilliant and sensitive,

and she loved reading more than anything in the world. Matilda went to school where she had a lovely teacher named Miss Honey. Unfortunately, the school had a horrid Headmistress named Miss Trunchbull who took great pleasure out of making the children—and the teachers—absolutely miserable. Over the course of the novel, clever Matilda has many adventures at the school and in the end, magical things begin to happen.

By this time, Dahl was more than seventy years old, and he was in poor health. He was often frustrated with his publishers and unhappy that he had not been knighted by the Queen.[16] Despite his frustrations, Dahl continued to write and he began to undertake significant philanthropic work, including giving money and equipment to children's hospitals and supporting organizations that encouraged children to read.

Early in 1990, Patricia Neal wrote to Felicity and Roald and asked if they could settle their differences. The divided family met at a birthday party for Theo. It was the last time they would meet together.

Later that year, Dahl became increasingly ill, and he was diagnosed with myelo-dysplastic anemia, a rare blood disorder.[17] The Dahls tried to keep up with social engagements and with the writing of a cookbook they had begun called *Memories with Food at Gypsy House*. But Roald Dahl was "without that lovely old bubbly energy that drives one to write books and drink gin and chase after girls," as he explained in a newsletter

Johnny Depp as Willy Wonka from the 2005 film
Charlie and the Chocolate Factory.

for young people.[18] He died on November 23, 1990, at the age of seventy-four. He is buried on a hillside at Gypsy House in Great Missenden, and his grave is visited regularly by those who loved his work.

After Dahl's death, Felicity wrote, "This huge and wonderful man showed boundless kindness to others. To me he was the greatest husband a woman could ever have. To all our children he was the greatest father and friend, and to so many children round the world, the greatest writer."[19]

While to some, he was temperamental and to others just downright difficult, Roald Dahl was loved by his family, who try to keep his memory alive. Today, there is a huge following for Dahl's work. Each year, there are books written about his life and new printings of his books. There have been several movies made of his works, including *James and the Giant Peach* (1996) and *Matilda* (1996), and the recent adaptation of *Charlie and the Chocolate Factory*, which was released in 2005, starring Johnny Depp as Willy Wonka. There is an exciting website dedicated to his life and works, as well as the Roald Dahl Museum and Story Center, which opened in Great Missenden in 2005.

Roald Dahl's memory lives on.

In His Own Words

The following are quotes from Roald Dahl from a variety of sources, including *Memories with Food at Gypsy House*, which he wrote with his second wife, Felicity Dahl; the memoir *My Year*; an interview with Todd McCormack, which can be found on the Official Roald Dahl Website; and other articles and interviews conducted by Kevin Nudd, Lisa Tuttle, and Justin Wintle over the years.

About his mother, Sofie Dahl:

Her memory was prodigious and nothing [that] ever happened to her in her life was forgotten. Embarrassing moments, funny moments, desperate moments were all recounted in every detail and we would listen enthralled.[1]

On the history of chocolate:

The dates themselves should be taught in school to every child. Never mind about 1066 William the Conqueror, 1087 William the Second. Such things are not going to affect one's life. But 1932 the Mars Bar and 1936 Maltesers, and 1937 the Kit Kat—these dates are milestones in history and should be seared into the memory of every child in the country.[2]

On sports:

I regard all forms of sport, whether the pupil is good at them or not, as being a most important part of character-building. Sport teaches sportsmanship as well as how to be a good loser, and it teaches a lot of other things besides.[3]

On the definition of a short story:

[My definition of a short story is the] old definition—a beginning, a middle and an end. It's a definite plot which progresses and comes to a climax, and the reader is fully satisfied when he's finished it. . . . Most of the so-called short story writers of today do not really write short stories. They write essays or mood pieces.[4]

On what it's like to write a book:

When you're writing it's rather like going on a very long walk, across valleys and mountains and things, and you get the first view of what you see and you write it down. Then you walk a bit further, maybe to the top of a hill, and you see something else, then you write that and you go on like that day after day, getting different views of the same landscape really. The highest mountain of the walk is obviously the end of the book because it's got to be the best view of them all, when everything comes together and you can look back and see everything you've done all ties up. But it's a very, very long, slow process.[5]

On living in the country:

I wouldn't live anywhere else except in the country, here. And, of course, if you live in the country, your work is bound to be influenced by it in a lot of ways.[6]

On writers who influenced him:

[Writers who have influenced me are] D. H. Lawrence, for some of his sentences and phrasing, not for his construction—his use of words. And Hemingway, for his construction. The master, really, of modern writing. . . . He taught all of us the value of the short sentence, using adjectives very, very carefully—in other words, hardly at all unless you really wanted it to mean something. And you didn't keep saying "wonderful" because it became meaningless. They're great secrets, those, and nobody ever did it before him, they just didn't.[7]

On writing about collections and collectors:

I suppose [that many of my short story characters were collectors and people with very particular tastes] because I'm enormously interested in a number of things and have a fair knowledge of pictures, furniture, wines, et cetera. They are all things I love. So I make use of them. It's no good writing about things you don't know about. That's basic. Greyhound racing was another of my loves. I used to breed racing greyhounds. I knew about them so I wrote about them.[8]

On the importance of reading:

I have a passion for teaching kids to become readers . . . to become comfortable with a book, not daunted. Books shouldn't be daunting, they should be funny, exciting and wonderful; and learning to be a reader gives a terrific advantage.[9]

On writing for children:

Writing for children . . . is much harder than writing for adults. Children don't have the concentration of adults, and unless you hold them from the first page, they're going to wander away and watch the [television] or do something else. They only read for fun; you've got to hold them.[10]

Chronology

1911—Harald and Sofie Dahl marry and settle in Llandaff, Wales.

1912—Astri Dahl is born.

1914—Alfhild Dahl is born.

1916—Roald Dahl, the only son of Harald and Sofie Dahl, is born on September 13.

1917—Else Dahl is born.

1918—The Dahl family moves to Radyr, Wales.

1920—Sister Astri Dahl dies in February. Harald Dahl dies in April. Sister Asta Dahl is born in August. The Dahl family moves back to Llandaff.

1922—Roald attends the Elmtree School in Llandaff.

1923—Roald attends the Llandaff Cathedral School.

1925—Roald attends St. Peter's Preparatory School in Weston-super-Mare, Somerset, England.

1929—Roald begins school at Repton, in Derby, England.

1934—Roald graduates from Repton. He joins the Public Schools' Exploring Society on a trip to Newfoundland. Upon his return, he begins work for Shell Oil Company in London.

1938—Dahl sets sail for Dar es Salaam in eastern Africa to continue his work for Shell Oil.

1939—War is declared and Dahl joins the British Royal Air Force in Nairobi, Kenya, where he is made a leading aircraftman.

1940—Dahl is promoted to pilot officer and sets off to join 80 Squadron in western Egypt near Libya. He crashes en route, sustains serious injuries, and spends several months recuperating in Alexandria, Egypt.

1941—In April, Dahl finally joins 80 Squadron in Greece, where he participates in the infamous Battle of Athens. After the squadron retreats to Haifa, Dahl suffers from blackouts and severe headaches as a result of his 1940 accident. He is sent home to England where he is promoted to flying officer, although he is unable to fly anymore.

1942—Dahl is sent to Washington, D.C., as an assistant air attaché at the British Embassy. The story "Shot Down over Libya" is printed in the *Saturday Evening Post*.

1943—Disney publishes *The Gremlins (A Royal Air Force Story by Flight Lieutenant Roald Dahl)*.

1945—The war ends. Dahl returns home to England where he focuses his energies on writing for adults.

1951—Dahl moves to New York.

1952—Dahl meets actress Patricia Neal at a dinner party given by writer Lillian Hellman.

1953—Dahl and Neal are married in New York City on July 2.

1955—Daughter Olivia is born. The family begins to travel back and forth to Great Missenden, England, where the rest of the Dahl family lives.

1957—Daughter Tessa is born.

1960—Theo, Dahl and Neal's only son, is born. The family returns to New York so Pat can begin filming *Breakfast at Tiffany's*. In December, Theo suffers a terrible accident when the baby carriage is hit by a taxicab. Doctors are unsure whether he will survive.

1961—Theo begins to recover and the family returns to England. *James and the Giant Peach* is published.

1962—The Wade-Dahl-Till Valve, a type of brain shunt, is patented in June. Fortunately, Theo continues to recover and he never actually needs to use the valve. Daughter Olivia dies from measles encephalitis on November 17.

1964—*Charlie and the Chocolate Factory* is published. Pat wins an Academy Award for her portrayal of Alma in the movie *Hud*. Daughter Ophelia is born.

1965—Pat suffers from several aneurysms while pregnant with their fifth child. She struggles to recover, which she does successfully after many years of hard work. Daughter Lucy is born healthy, five months after her mother's stroke.

1967—*You Only Live Twice*, a James Bond movie for which Dahl had written the screenplay, is released. Dahl's 82-year-old mother, Sofie, dies while he is in the hospital having surgery on his spine.

1971—The movie *Willy Wonka and the Chocolate Factory*, starring Gene Wilder as Willy Wonka, is released.

1972—Dahl meets Felicity (Liccy) Crosland.

1975—*Danny, the Champion of the World* is published. Dahl begins to work with illustrator Quentin Blake.

1982—*The BFG* is published.

1983—Dahl and Neal divorce. Dahl marries Felicity Crosland. *The Witches* is published.

1984—*Boy* is published.

1986—*Going Solo* is published.

1988—*Matilda* is published.

1990—Dahl dies on November 23 at age seventy-four and is buried in Great Missenden.

Selected Works

1943   *The Gremlins (A Royal Air Force Story by Flight Lieutenant Roald Dahl)*

1961   *James and the Giant Peach*

1964   *Charlie and the Chocolate Factory*

1966   *The Magic Finger*

1970   *Fantastic Mr. Fox*

1972   *Charlie and the Great Glass Elevator*

1975   *Danny, the Champion of the World*

1978   *The Enormous Crocodile*

1980   *The Twits*

1981   *George's Marvelous Medicine*

1982   *Revolting Rhymes*
        The BFG

1983   *Dirty Beasts*
        The Witches

1984   *Boy*

1985   *The Giraffe and the Pelly and Me*

1986   *Going Solo*

1988   *Matilda*

1990   *Esio Trot*

1991   *The Minpins*
        The Vicar of Nibbleswicke

1993   *My Year*

1994   *Revolting Recipes*

2001   *Even More Revolting Rhymes*

Chapter Notes

Chapter 1. A Child at Heart

1. Jeremy Treglown, *Roald Dahl: A Biography* (New York: Harcourt Brace & Co., 1994), p. 276.

Chapter 2. A Passion for Sweets and Adventure

1. Felicity and Roald Dahl, *Memories with Food at Gyspy House* (New York: Viking, 1991), pp. 154–155.
2. Roald Dahl, *Boy* (Middlesex, England: Puffin Books, 1984), p. 29.
3. Ibid., p. 33.
4. Ibid., pp. 29–52.
5. Ibid., pp. 147–148.
6. Ibid., p. 149.
7. Roald Dahl, *Charlie and the Chocolate Factory* (New York: Puffin Books, 1998), p. 64.

Chapter 3. The Family From Norway

1. Roald Dahl, *Boy* (Middlesex, England: Puffin Books, 1984), pp. 17–18.
2. Ibid., p. 12.
3. Ibid., p. 15.
4. Ibid., p. 16.
5. Felicity and Roald Dahl, *Memories with Food at Gypsy House* (New York: Viking, 1991), p. 65.
6. Ibid.

3. Ibid., p. 55. There is some question as to whether Dahl met Balfour or the Secretary of State, Sir Archibald Sinclair, since Dahl told the story differently to interviewers.
4. Ibid., p. 69.
5. Ibid., pp. 62–69.

Chapter 8. Marriage and Family

1. Barry Farrell, *Pat and Roald* (New York: Random House, 1969), p. 69.
2. Patricia Neal, *As I Am: An Autobiography* (New York: Simon and Schuster, 1988), p. 155.
3. Farrell, p. 125.
4. Neal, p. 189.
5. Ralph Steadman, "The Hut," *The Roald Dahl Treasury* (New York: Viking, 1997), p. 12.
6. Roald Dahl, *My Year* (London: Jonathan Cape Ltd, 1993), pp. 7–9.
7. "Roald Dahl Biography," *Official Roald Dahl Website*, n.d., <http://www.roalddahl.com>, (September 1, 2004).
8. Roald Dahl, *James and the Giant Peach* (New York: Puffin Books, 1961), p. 11.
9. Jeremy Treglown, *Roald Dahl: A Biography* (New York: Harcourt Brace & Co., 1994), p. 134.

Chapter 9. A Decade of Tragedy

1. Barry Farrell, *Pat and Roald* (New York: Random House, 1969), pp. 128–129.
2. Ibid., p. 128.
3. Jeremy Treglown, *Roald Dahl: A Biography* (New York: Harcourt Brace & Co., 1994), p. 144.
4. Roald Dahl, *Charlie and the Chocolate Factory* (New York: Puffin Books, 1964), p. 6.
5. Ibid., p. 9.

6. Patricia Neal, *As I Am: An Autobiography* (New York: Simon and Schuster, 1988), p. 231.

7. Treglown, p. 146.

8. Neal, p. 238.

9. Ibid., p. 247.

10. Treglown, p. 169.

11. Ibid., p. 173.

12. Mel Stuart with Josh Young, *Pure Imagination* (New York: LA Weekly Book for St. Martin's Press, 2002), p. 14.

13. Farrell, p. 213.

Chapter 10. A Writer's Empire and the End of an Era

1. Patricia Neal, *As I Am: An Autobiography* (New York: Simon and Schuster, 1988), p. 294.

2. Ibid., p. 320.

3. Jeremy Treglown, *Roald Dahl: A Biography* (New York: Harcourt Brace & Co., 1994), p. 209; Felicity and Roald Dahl, *Memories with Food at Gypsy House* (New York: Viking, 1991), p. 48.

4. Neal, p. 332.

5. Roald Dahl, *Danny, the Champion of the World* (New York: Bandam Skylark Book, 1975), p. v.

6. Treglown, p. 140.

7. Dahl, *Danny*, p. 150.

8. Ibid., p. 198.

9. Dahl, *Memories with Food*, p. 99.

10. *The Official Quentin Blake Website*, n.d., <http://www.quentinblake.com/about/interview3.htm>, (December 11, 2004).

11. Roald Dahl, *The BFG* (New York: Puffin Books, 1982), p. 48.

12. Treglown, p. 238.; *The Official Quentin Blake Website*, n.d., <http://www.quentinblake.com/about/interview4.htm>, (December 11, 2004).

13. Roald Dahl, *The Witches* (New York: Puffin Books, 1985), p. 12.

14. *The Witches* was made into a feature film, which was released in 1990.

15. Roald Dahl, *Matilda* (New York: Penguin Books, 1988), p. 10.

16. Treglown, p. 267.

17. "Roald Dahl Biography," *The Official Roald Dahl Website*, n.d., <http://www.roalddahl.com>, (September 1, 2004).

18. Ibid.

19. Dahl, *Memories with Food*, p. 11.

In His Own Words

1. Felicity and Roald Dahl, *Memories with Food at Gypsy House*, (New York: Viking, 1991), p. 68.

2. Ibid., pp. 154–155.

3. Roald Dahl, *My Year* (London: Jonathan Cape Ltd, 1993), p. 25.

4. Interview in 1974 with Justin Wintle for "The Pied Pipers: Interviews with the influential creators of children's literature," <http://www.roalddahlfans.com/articles/piedtext.php> (July 23, 2005).

5. Interview with Todd McCormack, *Official Roald Dahl Website*, n.d., <http://www.roalddahl.com> (July 23, 2005).

6. Ibid.

7. Interview with Lisa Tuttle for "Roald Dahl: His Style Is Witty, His Imagination's Nasty . . . and He Also Writes for Children," *The Twilight Zone Magazine*, February 1983, <http://www.roalddahlfans.com/articles/twilart.php> (July 23, 2005).

8. Interview in 1974 with Justin Wintle for "The Pied Pipers: Interviews with the influential creators of children's literature," <http://www.roalddahlfans.com/articles/piedtext.php> (July 23, 2005).

9. "Roald Dahl Biography," *Official Roald Dahl Website*, n.d., <http://www.roalddahl.com> (September 1, 2004).

10. Kevin Nudd, "The Children's Books of Roald Dahl." *Book and Magazine Collector*, January 1989, <http://www.roalddahlfans.com/articles/bmcjan89art.php> (July 23, 2005).

Glossary

aneurysm—A weak area in the wall of an artery that supplies blood to the brain. If the area ruptures, it can cause a stroke.

appendicitis—Inflammation of the appendix, a disease which is treatable today.

Askaris—Soldiers in the King's African Rifles, a group of African military men in the British army in World War II.

boazer—See *prefect*.

District Officers—Government officials in eastern Africa during colonial rule.

expatriate—An individual who takes up residence in a foreign country.

Fives—A game similar to handball in the United States, with a more complicated court and a more subtle points system. Roald Dahl played a version known as *Eton-Fives*.

fjords—Cliff-lined waterways which are found throughout Norway.

"glorious walk"—A walk in a beautiful setting, which Roald Dahl's father encouraged his wife to take when pregnant with their children.

gremlins—Fictional creatures whom soldiers blamed for problems which occurred on their planes. They were often described as small elves.

measles encephalitis—A rare form of the measles which is accompanied by an inflammation of the brain.

mpishi—Cook, in Swahili.

Myelo-dysplastic anemia—A rare blood disorder.

prefects— Students who organize house activities and study halls in boarding schools. Usually these students are older than their charges. At Roald Dahl's schools, they were also known as "boazers."

RAF—The British Royal Air Force.

Wade-Dahl-Till valve—A valve designed by Roald Dahl, Stanley Wade, and Kenneth Till, which was easier to insert into the brain and clogged less frequently than previously used valves. It was patented in 1962.

Further Reading

Books

Craats, Rennay. *Roald Dahl*. Mankato, Minn.: Weigl Publishers, Inc., 2002.

Hook, Jason. *Roald Dahl: The Storyteller*. Austin, Tex.: Raintree, 2004.

Rowley, John. *Roald Dahl: An Unauthorized Biography*. Chicago, Ill.: Heinemann Library, 1998.

Shields, Charles. *Roald Dahl*. Broomall, Pa.: Chelsea House, 2002.

Woog, Adam. *Roald Dahl*. Farmington Hills, Mich.: Kidhaven Press, 2004.

Internet Addresses

The Official Roald Dahl Website
  http://www.roalddahl.com/

Roald Dahl Fans Website
  http://www.roalddahlfans.com/

Roald Dahl: Teacher Resource Unit
  http://falcon.jmu.edu/~ramseyil/dahl.htm

Index